The Art of Modern War

Volume 1

Dan Green

Published by Profession Progression
www.ProfessionProgression.com
Copyright © 2013 by Dan Green
All rights reserved

THE ART OF MODERN WAR

For all the gremmies that are still searching for forever homes,

And for my Muse, My Precious.

THE ART OF MODERN WAR

The only way to predict the future is to create it

THE ART OF MODERN WAR

Cover Art by Ian Gillespie

THE ART OF MODERN WAR

Introduction

Sun Tzu was a master philosopher, strategist, and military general who lived during the Zhou dynasty, some 2500 years ago. Originally a military text of stratagem, *The Art of War* has influenced military and political leaders throughout the centuries. His ideas still hold true today and are highly applicable to the modern-day battleground…corporations.

Organizations have a collective psychology and oftentimes an underlying psychosis. Despite nearly 100 years of effort to make management a science, starting with Frederick Taylor in the early 1900s, organizations today are still composed of individuals and their feelings. Even though decisions that are made in everyday business are supposedly rooted in logic and rational thought, almost all decisions are ultimately judgments, and just like all of human behavior, those judgments are based on the individual's mood, feelings, and thoughts.

This volume is to be consumed in small chunks, and highlights 21 of Sun Tzu's most applicable strategies. It is aimed toward helping the individual to become a master of his or her surroundings, situations, and adversaries in a corporate environment.

THE ART OF MODERN WAR

This volume applies ancient philosophy to modern-day situations and highlights how we can influence the behavior of others by creating the environment we want, tapping into the feelings and thoughts of others, and ultimately impacting leadership judgments.

Some may call it manipulation, some may call it deception. I call it the Art of Modern War.

THE ART OF MODERN WAR

About the Author

Dan Green is an I/O psychology and organizational strategy consultant who has spent the last 15 years helping companies achieve their goals and align to their vision. Organizations he has accelerated toward success include BearingPoint, Deloitte, Stanley Associates, Tandberg, Cisco Systems, The Washington Capitals, eGreen LLC, Underground Audio, Four-leaf Design, Open Net Inc., Oberon Associates, and many others. His subject matter expertise is in customer success, improving the lives of individual employees, corporate finance, metric systems, global operations, ease of doing business, process engineering, value stream mapping, strategic planning, and increasing process velocities.

He holds an MBA from Marymount University and a BS in Business Management from George Mason, and his certifications include PMP, ITILv3 Expert, and Lean Six Sigma Black Belt, with subject matter expertise in Balanced Scorecard methodology, emotional intelligence, organizational behavior, global operations, sales enablement, and overall corporate ninja tactics.

He will receive his PhD in I/O psychology in 2014.

THE ART OF MODERN WAR

Volume 1

At the end of his resources	2
Releasing the trigger	7
The skillful soldier	11
Lengthy campaigns	14
Local guides	17
Truth of their reports	20
In all fighting	24
Too strong and too weak	27
Our position is unassailable	31
Give him no rest	35
A season for fire	38
Leave an outlet free	41
In our own hands	43
Crossing a river	45
Humble words	48
Different ground	50
Machiavellian for a day	53
Regulated by the infinite	57
Using fire to create	60

THE ART OF MODERN WAR

A country for old men — 64

Deception can make dreams come true — 68

At the end of his resources

The Army on the March #36

"Too frequent rewards signify that the enemy is at the end of his resources; too many punishments betray a condition of dire distress."

When an army is in distress, the fear of mutiny is always present. Lavish rewards are handed out to keep the men in good spirits, but this can only last for so long. Far too often, I see this situation in modern business and everyday life. It is the practice of addressing the surface-level symptom, rather than the underlying cause of the problem. Many companies today experience internal and external pain points just like every other company, which manifest themselves in the form of lower customer satisfaction scores, dropping employee motivation or retention, minimum levels of employee engagement, and lower revenues and profits. One of the advantages of studying and applying Industrial and Organizational psychology is the ability to examine these pain points by observing the overall psychology and psychosis of the organization. By understanding that organizations have a personality, we can apply a method of psychological analysis to treat the symptoms of the organizational psychosis. I understand that this may be a bit of a stretch for some of you, so let me backtrack a bit.

As I mentioned in the introduction, despite the nearly 100 years of effort to make management a science, started by Frederick Taylor in the early 1900s, organizations today comprise of individuals and their feelings. Even though decisions that are made in everyday business are supposedly rooted in logic and rational thought, almost all decisions are ultimately judgments, and just like all of human behavior, those judgments are based on the individual's mood, feelings, and thoughts. The way in which the employee feels about the organization, and the organization about the employee, is the genesis of psychological and organizational dysfunction that eventually manifests itself into the surface-level problems I mentioned earlier.

The organization itself also possesses a collective personality and seeks equilibrium with all forces that act upon it, internally and externally. This equilibrium is often sought in haste, which results in poor or wrong management decisions about the forces that are causing the imbalance.

OK, enough psychology.

"Too frequent rewards" does indeed signify that management isn't paying attention to the processes that underpin these pain points and the practices that perpetuate them, but rather hoping to solve the business issues at the surface level. Here are some examples of things I have seen that management hoped would cure low employee motivation and satisfaction:

- Hand out T-shirts and company key chains
- Increases in salary (small ones)
- Company outings
- Forced rotations to other roles

Ask yourself, if you were truly unhappy in your role, would any of these "rewards" change that? No, not even the increase in salary would. Rather than trying to drill down to the root cause of the dissatisfaction, what management viewed as "rewards" were thrown at employees in an attempt to boost satisfaction. Sometimes there are better efforts undertaken that have been proven in the general landscape, such as recognition programs and career pathing, but the application is still generalized and not tailored to the individual personalities of the organization. This would be like a doctor giving you a general treatment for your rash without examining you first. I'm not a medical doctor, but I suspect there are many things that can cause a similar looking rash. Each person is unique, and so is the root of his or her dissatisfaction or loss of motivation. Organizations that do not understand this often try to shower their employees with many rewards, signifying desperation.

Too frequent rewards signify that the organization is at the end of their resources.

In this context, the resources could be ideas, management's ability to lead, or innovation. Regardless of how we apply the term "resources" in the modern context, it always is a mistake that also could signify the end for many companies. "Too many punishments" is also the same. When organizations are quick to layoffs or quick to place blame, it is the same practice in reverse. Rather than trying to understand the processes and problems that got you to this point, only the surface level issues are "addressed," and many are baffled when the problems continue.

How can this be applied in our daily lives? Let's look at challenges that we face today in our careers, our relationships, and our lives. Rather than throw too many rewards at it, let's try to understand the underlying and often hidden processes that are perpetuating these challenges. An iceberg analogy would be too easy here, but you get the point. Let's dig down below the surface, and understand what caused this pain point and address that part of the problem, rather than trying to eliminate the surface problem itself with too many rewards.

Remember, behavior and judgments are based on feeling and thought. Dig deep, and try to discover the "why" first.

Releasing the trigger

Energy #15

"Energy may be likened to the bending of a crossbow; decision, to the releasing of the trigger."

A simple illustration highlighting the differences between types of energy. Energy can be both potential and kinetic. The bending of a crossbow represents potential energy, stored and ready to be released. The release of the trigger represents kinetic energy, which is the movement associated with the arrow. Without getting too scientific, you cannot have one without the other, and your kinetic energy is a direct consequence of the amount of potential energy that is stored.

Both types of energy need to be handled and respected in total concert, if the arrow is to hit the target successfully the first time. Not bending the bow and storing the energy at the right time may mean a missed opportunity; the premature release of the trigger may result in a missed target. Both types of energy must work together for a successful outcome to occur.

We see many organizations today that are normally very good at potential or kinetic, but rarely good at both. Potential can be synonymous with caution, the storing of energy for when it is needed. But cautious companies that do not take risks merely always have the bow bent, and rarely know when, if at all, to release the trigger. In modern economic times, especially in times of recession, companies lean more toward potential energy because of fear and indecision.

This is the wrong approach.

Let's think back to the years 1929--1933, the Great Depression. People were not buying much, but refrigerator sales went up 30%. It was a highly innovative product at the time, but the refrigerator industry took the risks to invest in R&D, hire people, and market the product. Many others industries were not doing any of this; they had the bow bent, waiting for the Depression to pass. What really passed them was opportunity.

Do not let your environment or any outside factors influence your decision to release the trigger.

The opposite is also true. Some companies love to take risks and love the idea of movement and kinetic energy so much that their timing is often incorrect or their energy isn't stored properly to make the right decisions.

There is no focus on the potential, and there is no focus on storing the proper amount of energy so that the arrow is on target the first time. We see this very often in the restaurant industry. Out of 10 restaurants, 9 fail for a variety of reasons, but they all have one common theme: they focus on the daily task, the hustle and bustle of providing the meals to the customer *that* day. The kinetic energy is abundant, but there is very little planning around cost control, market space, and brand. No energy is stored for larger or more strategic tasks, so the focus remains on the surface level, the daily interaction, the kinetic. The bow needs to be bent and the energy stored, only to be released at the precise time that will ensure success. Sure, you can fire many arrows and have massive kinetic energy, but if you only hit the target once, is that success? If you lose a hundred arrows in the process, is that success?

Success lies in the ability to store energy and to release energy, and in the ability to be decisive and knowledgeable about timing. Too much potential energy with no release amounts to nothing; too much kinetic with no proper storage amounts to failure. As workers, managers, leaders, and citizens of society, our success will be determined by the ability to store the proper amount of energy and the ability to release the energy at the right time, the first time.

Become a master of both the potential and the kinetic, and your arrow will always fly true.

THE ART OF MODERN WAR

The skillful soldier

Waging War #8

"The skillful soldier does not raise a second levy, neither are his supply-wagons loaded more than twice."

I've said it before and I'll say it again…organizations are attack devices. Far too often, soldiers and generals have a backup plan or contingency. What happens if our first plan doesn't work? What happens if the battle doesn't go as planned or the enemy doesn't respond as predicted? What this wisdom tells us is that there is no need for contingency if the soldier is skillful enough to dictate the terms of battle and the outcome of the war before it begins.

A second levy suggests that the soldier didn't do his homework to KNOW where the attack is coming from, and a third supply-wagon load suggests that he isn't confident that the first attack will be all that is necessary. If you read the wisdom closely, it says don't fill more than twice. I believe this to be true for the sole reason that you don't want to exhaust all of your resources on the initial attack, but the second should **only** have enough to bring you back from the dead.

Do your research. Put all your resources into your first and only attack, with a minimal amount to resurrect you if needed.

Contingency planning and third supply-wagons not only take up resources and mental bandwidth, but they also place a seed of doubt in your mind while simultaneously reducing your strength. You become your own worst enemy, so why do that to yourself? Your external enemies would love to reduce your strength, confidence, and will power. Don't do it for them. The business world is full of negative stakeholders and people who want to see you fail. Make sure your attack is on point and to the fullest extent of your ability.

Have the confidence to know where to attack, and to know that you only need to attack once. If you fail, it is most likely a symptom of poor planning or poor methodology. Either way, you will have the ability to regroup and plan again; just don't do your secondary planning beforehand. Put all of your effort into making your first attack, your first presentation, your first impression, or your first sales pitch, be the best that it can possibly be, so that not only will you not have to resupply your wagons, but you will most likely have some initial supplies left over.

General George S. Patton offered some insight into this topic when he spoke to the Third Army on the night before the Allied invasion of France in 1944: "I don't want to receive any messages saying that we are holding our position. We are not holding a goddamned thing. Let the Germans do that. We are advancing constantly…we advance over, under, or through the enemy. We are going to go through him like crap through a goose."

I have a feeling your next work meeting will kick ass.

Lengthy campaigns

Waging War #19

"In war, then, let your great object be victory, not lengthy campaigns."

How many consultants does it take to change a light bulb? We don't know; they never seem to get past the feasibility study…

That's an example of one of the many jokes out there highlighting the general perception of consultants everywhere. The idea is that consultants merely drag out problems, suck their clients dry by the hour, and prolong problems to ensure "job security". Whether or not many consultants live by this philosophy today, I think it is a very important lesson from Sun Tzu, and I am glad I will be the one translating this ancient lesson for you.

Job security is not based on longevity. Far too often, I witness consultants, contractors, employees, and other various paid individuals approach work with the mindset that their great object of victory is to prolong their employment by working slowly, not sharing vital knowledge, or putting in the minimum amount of effort required. I understand the notion that some may feel that their unique knowledge or ability is what locks in their employment status, or that the longer they drag their feet on a project, they will continue to receive those paychecks. While this nearsighted approach may do just that, it sends a different message to an employer. It sends a message about your value.

Value is the way to secure jobs, employment, positions, and contracts. Value is determined by return on investment, which is a simple calculation of time and money. *Time is money.* When I consult on any project, my fees are fixed and value based. I never charge by the hour. My fee is based on a simple calculation of how long I feel it will take me, what I feel my hourly rate should be, and the return the employer receives on their investment in me. This formula usually helps me determine the financial impact I am bringing my client, with my fees being twenty times less than that. An example would be if I feel my efforts will save my client $1,000,000, I will charge $50,000. And I will communicate one date that I will be finished, but strive to finish way before it. *Under promise and over deliver.* Being able to consistently deliver an ROI of over twenty times makes me an easy sell for the next gig, gives me measurable and provable value, and gives me more job security than any molasses-paced work output would. This is an easy formula that can work for you too, in any line of work you are in.

Make your great object be victory…a fast victory.

Under promise and over deliver. If you tell your boss that you will be done in 20 days, be done in 15. Your value will skyrocket. Share your knowledge to demonstrate that you are the expert and have the ability to enable your organization toward achieving desired business outcomes. Don't bend them over a barrel by holding onto your knowledge and assume that this makes people want to work with you and that the organization views you as an asset. *This doesn't create value, it creates dependency.* Let's not confuse the two; organizations keep valuable people. Organizations are always searching for ways to automate and eliminate their dependencies or find cheaper alternatives.

Another tangent about time and money. One of them you can make more of, infinitely more of; the other is lost forever as it is spent. You can always make another dollar; you can never make another minute. Get into the mindset that your most valuable possession is your time. When you deliver with quickness and ninja-like speed, you are giving managers, leaders, and organizations their time back.

I can't imagine what would make you more valuable than that.

Local guides

Maneuvering #14

"We shall be unable to turn natural advantages to account unless we make use of local guides."

Global Reach, Local Touch. This is often forgotten, and the price for forgetting this is steep.

As technology and the Internet shrink the world into a single global marketplace, oftentimes the success of major corporations comes with blinders for its leadership. Powerful brands that have been created and the success of the product or service in the markets they are currently in give company leaders a sense of arrogance, laziness, or both. This little tidbit of wisdom is the most important aspect of globalization, in my opinion, and one that is far overlooked. Anyone who has been to business school is bombarded with these types of case studies, so I will give you two of my favorite examples.

A major player in the shampoo industry found out this lesson the hard way. Assuming their global presence was strong enough to compel any market to purchase their products, the company started to sell shampoo in Asia, only to find sales to be dismal after the first cycle. The leadership and company executives were puzzled as to why the shampoo wouldn't sell, and used their large cash reserves to conduct feasibility studies, market analyses, penetration statistics, and so on. After millions of dollars spent and no clear-cut answers, they finally decided to seek a local guide. They discovered that it was the behavior of consumers in Asia to frequently try new shampoo brands, so they only liked to purchase small bottles. The American shampoo company had stocked the Asian shelves with "normal" size bottles, but the Asian consumers did not want to make such a large commitment. No market study or analysis would have yielded this tacit and undocumented buying behavior, and leadership learned the hard way that their natural brand advantage was nothing without the help of local guides.

My second example is that of Gerber, who decided to expand their product into the emerging market of Africa. Every American is familiar with Gerber and what the jar of baby food looks like. It has a nice little picture of a baby on the front, and the brand is unmistakable. After thorough market analysis and study, Gerber decided to enter the African market, assuming that a low-cost baby food would instantly become a product leader. Sales were dismal to non-existent at first. What Gerber failed to realize is that in most countries in Africa, the local population can't read English, or read at all, so it is customary to put a picture of what is inside the jar, on the outside of it, so they could know what they are about to eat.

Gerber has a baby on the outside of their jar...

You can easily see how the brand prowess, the low-cost differentiation, and the global reach were nothing when not combined with local touch.

Many of us don't have global brands. I understand that. But this bit of wisdom from *The Art of War*, combined with examples of real-world failures, should get your gears turning. In your next sales call, production meeting, or performance review, don't let the fact that you kick ass be your only weapon. Take time to understand the local scene. This local scene could simply be knowing the state traditions that your customer lives in, the company policy on promotions, or the cultural perceptions of your production team. Certainly take time to develop your global reach, your global power, and a dominating personal brand.

But never lose sight that it can easily crumble when you don't account for the local way of doing things.

Truth of their reports

The Use of Spies #17

"Without subtle ingenuity of mind, one cannot make certain of the truth of their reports."

This may seem like an obvious one, but it's something that I run into almost every day. People in their daily lives and managers in their organizations take potentially life-changing information at face value merely because they see it with their own eyes. It's funny to me that you need to remind people that not everything you read on the Internet is true. My favorite quote that exemplifies this is…

"67% of the quotes you read online are false." – Abraham Lincoln

In business, metrics are leadership's view into the health of the operation. Everything, from how the customers feel, to how the employees feel, to how the company is doing financially, is (or should be) quantitatively measured and expressed in some visual representation such as a graph, balance sheet, or report. These metrics drive the behavior of leadership and are used as guidance to make decisions that change the path of the business and people's lives. Very rarely though are the sources of these metrics verified for accuracy. Many organizations do not invest in the tools and expertise necessary to have automated metrics reporting, so the reports are generated as raw data dumps and then pivoted and manipulated manually by a human. The inaccuracy that comes from human error, personal agenda, and political landscape all play into the manually crafted reports, and even though leadership should use some ingenuity to verify the numbers, oftentimes, they don't.

People do the same thing. How often have you heard something from a friend about what someone else said or did, and before you could actually verify the truth, you developed strong feelings about the report? Rumors, innuendo, spoken and written word, and other forms of communication all come with much more layering and complexity than what is actually communicated at the surface level. It is up to each of us to verify the information and to question the source of the information before plotting any course of action or making any business decisions.

I am not saying that you should be skeptical of everyone and that you shouldn't trust anyone. Or am I? When most people think about trust, they merely think of trust as "do I believe that this person is telling me the truth?" This needs to be taken a step further. When you think of trust, you need to think of each and every resulting action that happens as a result of that report. Let me give you an example.

I receive a report that says our customers haven't been happy for four quarters: do I believe the report is accurate? Yes, the analyst is very good at his job, so I trust it is accurate.

Because of this report, I need to fire my Director of Customer Experience because I anticipate that our stock will take a major hit if I don't react quickly. Now, here is where the level of trust needs to cascade. Do I trust my analyst ENOUGH to believe in his report, AND substantiate all of the resulting action because of the report? If the answer is no, then I need to verify. This may be a cynical view of the world, but I'll be honest, I don't trust many people. I can count the number on one hand. Not because I don't think others would tell me the truth, because most of my peers do. It's that I don't trust the information they give me *enough* to give me a clear conscience all the way through major decisions that I would need to make in my work and in my life. Unless you trust the report enough to believe its accuracy and all of the resulting actions that will come of it, it needs to be verified first. With a little ingenuity, one can verify all the reports received, but still not offend everyone that you "don't trust."

Use your spies wisely, as they are of great advantage in business and in life, but always remember that one must first understand what the information is saying and understand what actions will result from it before making any major decisions. As a friend of mine always says, "I don't lie, I just willfully contribute to the campaign of misinformation."

Make sure that you trust the source, and that you understand the outcomes that the information and subsequent actions will create.

In all fighting

Energy #5

"In all fighting, the direct method may be used for joining battle, but indirect methods will be needed in order to secure victory."

Some people are merely concerned with joining the battle and often it is "monkey see, monkey do." In war, the direct method will be engagement on the battlefield or other obvious methods, with your chances of success boiling down to a mixture of luck and resources. While modern business is not often life and death as it is on the battlefield, I personally wouldn't want my victory to be based on luck and resources alone.

Within this wisdom, we will assume that the word "direct" means that it is the same method that everyone else is doing. Companies all over the world are constantly copying each other and engaging in direct methods, mainly because they are solely focused on joining the battle and assume their success will be based on producing similar products and services but in a more cost-efficient way. Often, this is not the case, and the consumer is left with multiple companies that give out very similar products or services, with no real differentiators to speak of.

This is not victory.

So how do we actually secure victory? Indirect methods, or doing something that no one else is doing, are what will bring ultimate success.

We hear corporate buzzwords such as "innovation" all the time, but there is a strong meaning to it that has been lost in recent years. J.B. Woods wrote in his books, *Complexity Avalanche* and *Consumption Economics*, about a phenomenon that is occurring in the technology services economy today. To summarize, he goes to great lengths to describe how customers are no longer locked into massive software solutions because of their heavy upfront investment, but rather have the ability to shop around and choose services *à la carte* from many different vendors online. Earlier, companies could rely on the large upfront investment of their customer as a massive exit barrier and didn't need to focus on innovation or indirect methods to be successful. With the rise of software-on-demand and cloud-based solutions, this is no longer the case.

Obviously, direct methods are direct for a reason. They have proven to be effective in the past, but that doesn't mean they are the best way to secure victory. I am not saying that companies need to fly off the chain and take innovation to a crazy extreme, but the ability to craft indirect solutions and be creative in their customer engagement models is the key difference between merely joining the battle and emerging as the victor. Innovation cannot succeed without a strong base of core business principles and models, but those core practices alone will only ensure you are a market participant, not guarantee that you are a market leader.

When developing your own personal brand, think about the value that you have to offer and what makes you unique. The perfect combination of direct and indirect methods will be the key in establishing your value, justifying your next salary, and convincing your next customer that they should go with you instead of your competitor.

Join the battle and battle well, but think about what makes you different and what you can do differently and victory will be yours.

Too strong and too weak

Terrain #16

"When the common soldiers are too strong and their officers too weak, the result is insubordination. When the officers are too strong and the common soldiers too weak, the result is collapse."

Armies rely on the total and uniform strength of their ranks. Their success isn't based on having the *same* strengths, but *uniform* strengths. There is a major difference between the two. Organizations and groups actually thrive on diversity and possessing unique abilities. This is a fact that has been proven, so having different strengths is vital to success. It is the imbalance of strength and power that will tip the organizational psyche toward insubordination or collapse.

It's the whole "weakest link in the chain" idea, but unfortunately, armies and organizations are much more complex than a single line of looped steel.

The term "top heavy" in modern business refers to the organizational situation where there are large numbers of managers, directors, and executives. In modern economic times, many companies are struggling financially because the officers are too strong and the common soldiers are too weak. The common soldiers are weak in numbers, motivation, skills, and pay, which leads to a poor end product or service. According to recent studies, the median CEO salary is $9.587 million in America. According to Associated Press calculations, the national median salary is $39,312. That means that the average worker would need to work for 244 years to make the median CEO salary. That's not to say that there absolutely needs to be financial parity between executive salaries and employee salaries, but when there are an equal number of executives as lower-level employees in an organization, you can see how this leads to collapse when the financial cost of the officers is so high. This is just an example to show the disparity between the soldiers' and officers' pay, and one can easily glean how corporations can be headed toward financial collapse when the officers are too strong and the soldiers are too weak. There needs to be a balance of strength and numbers, otherwise corporations become top heavy, bloated, and sluggish. This creates disenchanted employees and missed market opportunities, which means workers and customers will go elsewhere.

Make sure that the officers are not too strong.

The flip side is also true, but not so much in a financial sense. When the soldiers are too strong and the officers are too weak, insubordination occurs because of the lack of leadership and direction. Soldiers rule the coop and are too focused on daily activities, with no higher-level vision or strategic direction. Companies that focus too much on soldier strength put all of their efforts into their daily processes and products, and pay little attention to external forces and customer expectations. These are the areas where officer strength is key, because it ensures that organizational processes stay relevant to the times and customer mood swings. Soldiers are efficient in the production of the processes they are enlisted to do, and their sole focus should be on the optimization and creation of the final product or service. Focusing on bolstering this strength alone ensures that the organization develops blinders to the outside world and that the soldiers' work functions are considered the most important. This eventually leads to a sense of entitlement and disparity in the work force. Insubordination occurs when the soldiers are given too much power, and the officers are weak.

Make sure that the soldiers are not too strong.

Organizations are living organisms, with their own personality and psychology. They constantly look to balance the external forces that act upon them in the pursuit of homeostasis, so it is important to have balance from within. Any external balancing initiatives will fail if the balance of power internally is off center, and the organization will tip off the competitive landscape completely. Organizations, like armies, can ensure their success by striving for uniform power. Management needs to set clear strategy and direction for the organization, and the soldiers need to have the capabilities and skill set to create differentiation and competitive advantage in the market space. Strength that tips too far in either direction will lead to collapse or insubordination, both of which translate to failure.

Diversity of strength, equality of strength. That should be your organizational ideal.

Our position is unassailable

Variation of Tactics #11

"The Art of War teaches us to rely not on the likelihood of the enemy's not coming, but on our own readiness to receive him; not on the chance of his not attacking, but rather on the fact that we have made our position unassailable."

This is a great quote from *The Art of War* as it brings to life a common practice of modern business and everyday life. Our preparations, actions, and positions of power should not be built upon the probabilities of our external environment, but rather based on our own strengths. Unfortunately, too many people today rely on external factors instead of their own internal readiness.

This line from *The Art of War* highlights why it is dangerous to live for future events and not focus on the current state or the now, as it talks about individuals and companies that base their strategy and their actions on the likelihood or probability of others performing certain actions.

No one can predict the future.

Letting your path be guided by guessing what an external future scenario may be is a sure way to come up short. No one knows what our friends, family, competitors, or allies are going to do, and our positions of strength should not be based on those undetermined and often unlikely paths.

Focus inward on your own development and build your own strength.

Fear the known and leave the unknown alone. Build your internal capability to the point of being unassailable and bolster your strength to be able to receive ANY attack, not just the ones you think you see coming. This is applicable in personal lives and in your individual careers. There is no reason to waste precious energy on preparing for a future external scenario that may or may not occur.

Look at some of the best companies in the world today and some of the most successful individuals.

Do Apple, Google, and Walmart determine their strategic direction based off what others "might" do to their lines of business? Or do they build upon their own innovation and strength and cement their positions in the market space to the point of being unassailable?

Look at obvious successful individuals such as Warren Buffett, Fred Smith and Richard Branson. Buffett only invests in areas of his own knowledge and expertise and rarely invests in things he doesn't fully understand, regardless of what advisors or the marketplace tells him to do. Branson started his first business in the crypt of a church and named it Virgin because none of his workers had any knowledge of business. Fred Smith got a "C" on his term paper about FedEx and his professor said "it could never happen". We all know how that story turned out. They built upon their own internal strengths, went about things in their own way, and didn't worry about what external possibilities may or may not occur.

While some may say that preparing for the future is always prudent, I disagree when the context is based on a future construct that isn't guaranteed to occur. We do know with 100% certainty that we can enhance our own skills and power to develop an agile and solid presence, but we do not know with any certainty what enemies will do and how those actions will affect us.

Let your actions and your direction be guided by internal readiness, not external probabilities.

Build upon your internal strengths and positions of power, so that your castle moat runs deep and your fortress walls are solid. Prepare to effectively receive ALL forms of attack, not just the ones you think will occur.

Eventually, other people will start to prepare for you coming, and we all know how that will turn out for them.

Give him no rest

Laying Plans #23

"If he is taking his ease, give him no rest."

Good things come to those who wait? Or do we strike while the iron is hot? There are many contradictory folklore sayings, and each of them could be right in their own unique situations. The Japanese have a saying, *"keisu bai keisu"*, which means case by case. Do birds of a feather flock together or do opposites attract? Are two heads better than one or do too many cooks spoil the broth? Most of the time, it's *keisu bai keisu*; however, in business and in war, one should never wait and one should always strike while the iron is hot.

Waiting is a lazy man's game. Good things do not come your way, *they pass you by*. Think of where you are at this exact moment in life, and trace back how you got there. Look at all the major turning points in your life, and you can usually trace each instance to a circumstance of unique timing.

Timing is everything.

The night you met your significant other, the current career you have, and your good and bad luck can all boil down to your hard work, preparation, and your timing. Would these good things have come to you if you had waited? Or did you need to strike while the iron was hot? The key is being prepared for the moment and then pouncing when it does, not waiting for a better moment to come.

Now if you were GUARANTEED a better outcome by waiting, then sitting idle may be the best course, but last I checked, none of us could predict the future. Waiting not only delays the inevitable outcome of the situation, but keeps the dice rolling and the gamble going, all while spending the most valuable, nonrenewable source of wealth we possess…our time. We can never make another moment, so if we are not guaranteed a better outcome by waiting, then I ask you…why wait?

If our enemies or competitors are resting, there is no better time to pounce. If our goals present themselves to us, or our dreams could be realized in a fractional capacity, waiting around for the complete package will only leave you disappointed, confused, and empty handed.

We are all in competition. For resources, jobs, sales, mates, and time. That's not saying you need to bulldoze your friends along the way to get what you want, but if you don't take it in this life, are you waiting for someone to give it to you?

Give him no rest. Strike while the iron is hot, carpe diem, and all that warm fuzzy stuff. We've heard it all before. But how many of us are actually doing it? While competitors are resting, step up and snag what you know they desire.

Or wait around, let your enemies recover, and hope that something good comes your way…or passes you by.

A season for fire

The Attack by Fire #3

"There is a proper season for making attacks with fire, and special days for starting a conflagration."

A fire must not begin recklessly or haphazardly. A fire is easily started and sometimes impossible to contain and can be devastating to everything in its path. Attacking by fire should never be out of despair, disdain, or discomfort. Despite its relative ease and tremendous impact, its use should be the most delicate decision that you make. There is a proper season or proper time to use fire. However, there are those special days where you need to just burn it to the ground.

When we decide our methods of attack, there is always one thing that we need to ask ourselves first. *What do we want when the attack is over?* Most of us are so blinded by the vision of our enemy's defeat that we fail to think of what is next. If we want to acquire a company, a fortress, or a battlefield, we don't want to decimate it in our pursuit, unless our plan is to rebuild it anyway. If our intent is the total destruction of our competition, fire will do the trick, but who is to say the fire won't destroy us as well?

There is a proper season for making attacks with fire.

Fire can serve as a metaphor for our most powerful weapon, actions, strategy, or plan. The sheer fact of its power, and the events that it will set in motion afterwards, are the very reasons that a preferred season for its deployment exists. We must be aware of our environment, such as the temperature, the wind direction, and the rainfall, if we are to have a successful attack. Too many times in modern business, large companies use their brand of fire to crush opponents, only to have the flames burn most of what they were trying to acquire in the first place.

Recently, a major Fortune 50 company acquired a small technology firm with haste and swiftness, to take hold of the technology that this company strategically viewed as a gateway to the future. Not understanding the "seasons," the acquisition went through quickly and the larger company got the technology, only to realize that 95% of the smaller company workforce was "burned" in the acquisition process. The departure of these employees left the Fortune 50 company with a new technology that they not only did not know how to use, but also no longer had the people who did. Their haphazard deployment of fire torched the very thing they came for.

However, sometimes everything does just need to burn. If that is our goal, of course.

A conflagration is a firefighter's worst nightmare. It is a fire of devastating proportion. If the object of your victory is the decimation of your opponents, then there are special days for a conflagration. Just know that it is much harder to rebuild than to destroy, so put some thought into saving your big guns for when they are truly necessary. In your personal life and your career, attacks by your personal brand of fire can and will be easy to start and destroy quickly; just make sure the seasons are right, or the winds could turn it right back on you, destroying the very thing you are after.

I bet you are probably like me…and I love to play with matches every now and then.

Leave an outlet free

Maneuvering #36

"When you surround an army, leave an outlet free."

This may seem counterintuitive. If we have made a successful effort to surround an army, why would we give them a way to escape? The object of victory is to crush our enemies while preserving as many of our own resources as we can. By leaving an outlet free, we merely let them think they have an escape, when in reality they do not.

Animals, people, teams, and organizations often give their best defense in a fight when it is out of despair. You will usually get your opponent's strongest fight when they are backed into a corner with no escape. Providing an outlet for them to flee not only eliminates the despair from their defense, it also makes them reallocate mental and physical resources to their escape plan, making it easier for you to defeat them.

This tactic also has roots in organizational behavior. Organizational behavior is the practice of designing processes, programs, policies, and environments that create and sustain predictable behaviors from our work force and our competition. Companies that are considered top-notch innovators of the customer experience often have behavior predictability down to a science.

Despair equals unpredictability.

We never know how an enemy will react when they are backed into a corner because their defense will be their most powerful when fueled by despair. Make them believe they have a way out. By leaving an outlet free, we can predict their behavior and ensure a swift victory, since we will crush them when they flee in pursuit of their predictable path to freedom.

I prefer the fleeing enemy, distracted by a false escape path, than a rabid cornered beast, focusing all of its energy on me. No qualms about shooting a fleeing enemy in the back right? I certainly don't have any…

In our own hands

Tactical Dispositions #2

"To secure ourselves against defeat lies in our own hands, but the opportunity of defeating an enemy is provided by the enemy himself."

Offense wins games, defense wins championships. This saying is often misunderstood. People assume it means that "defense wins championship *games*" (as in the final game of the season or tournament). While offense is needed to put points on the board and win each *individual game*, defense is a *total concept* applying to the overall campaign, because in most sporting tournaments, if you lose once, you are done. So in our path to glory, it takes many games (offense) to win but only one game (defense) to lose. Hence, offense wins games, defense wins championships.

When listening to any war general, battle commander, sports gladiator, or cage fighter, all of their victory speeches have a common theme. Their path to victory wasn't paved through a blind onslaught of their own strengths onto enemy forces, but rather an exploitation of their enemy's specific weaknesses. To secure ourselves against defeat, the defense lies in our own hands. Our viability depends on the elimination, or at least concealment of our weaknesses, and our victory resides with the illumination and capitalization of our enemy's shortcomings. If we look closely, our enemy's, opponent's, or competitor's weakness is almost always provided to us by them.

In modern business, the same theory can apply. It takes a lifetime to build up a good reputation, but a single moment to destroy one. Think of each sales call, proposal, and executive presentation as a game, where a strategic offense is needed to win that particular event and move closer to your championship parade ending at the CEO office. But know that it only takes one loss to be eliminated. If we understand that the keys to victory lie in the exploitation of weakness, we must make a conscious effort to disguise our own and prey upon those of others. Knowing how you compare to the other people in the interview room, how your product stacks up against the competitors, or how your presentation lacks information that your coworker's has, enables us to conceal, address, or eliminate those shortcomings to ensure we win that specific game. It is a double-edged sword that cuts both ways, and understanding how the blade slices in each direction ensures we don't get cut.

Conceal your own weaknesses, pounce quickly upon theirs. You do the cutting. Cut and conceal, baby, cut and conceal.

Crossing a river

The Army on the March #3

"After crossing a river, you should get far away from it."

In ancient warfare, armies on the march often plodded for countless miles through untouched forests and unmapped terrain. After marching for days, sometimes they would come upon a river that they had no other choice but to cross. Turning back was not an option, and there was no telling how far the river stretched. It was usually the biggest obstacle a marching army faced, and one that gave the least amount of warning to its presence. Generals had to make tough decisions over how to cross, calculating loss of men, horses, supplies, and time lost. Armies would be weak after finally getting across, and enemies often knew this.

By the time an entire army reached the other side, their muscles were tired and their horses were exhausted. Half of the supplies could be lost and some men swept away, but the survivors often congratulated themselves for a challenge well completed and rested for the night on the other side of the river. Enemies understood this behavior and often attacked at this point. Not only was the river crossing army not at full strength, but with the river at their back, they had no escape. Throughout many wars in history, this strategy was often employed, and many major battles were lost right by a river.

The only way for the army to survive was to cross the river and get as far away from it as quickly as they could.

In modern times, we often have our own daily "rivers" to cross. We operate according to plan but sometimes stumble upon a river or challenge that we didn't see coming or have time to plan for. Being the ninjas we are, we often get through the challenge, sometimes with depleted resources, and have a tendency to sit on the other side patting ourselves on the back. This is the opportune time for our opponents to strike. While congratulations are often in order for a job well done, ensure that you aren't in a position of vulnerability before you celebrate. In today's business environments, timing, speed, velocity, and quickness are key differentiators to our success, and competitors know this. We could be patting ourselves on the back for a job well done, while others decimate us while we are weakened, not looking, or not paying attention to anything other than our recent river crossing victory.

In modern day sports such as ice hockey and soccer, it is universally known that your opponent has their best chance to score on you right after you just scored on them. Coincidence? I think not.

Revel in your accomplishments; just don't sit on the other side of the river for too long. Get away from it as fast as you can.

On the flip side, time your attacks for when your enemies are resting after crossing their rivers and you will be victorious.

Humble words

The Army on the March #24

"Humble words and increased preparations are signs that the enemy is about to advance. Violent language and driving forward as if to attack are signs that he will retreat."

Warfare is won and lost through deception. That is the whole premise of *The Art of War*. In modern business, deception is used to compete, as all companies are in competition for the same markets, the same dollars, and the same status levels. Through media and other avenues, companies can express their voice, and we can often glean from the posturing of their position what situations they are trying to conceal, and their subsequent behavior can often be predicted.

Think back to high school and the after-school fights that now seem silly. In a general sense, the loudest kids were the ones that had no intention of actually fighting, but needed to posture as loudly and violently as they could, in hopes that the situation would defuse. The ones who didn't say a word were the ones you needed to worry about (not that I got into any high school fights, this is just what I heard).

Positions of strength speak for themselves. The strongest of leaders and the most powerful humans speak softly and rely on their positions of strength to convey their intentions. That whole "speak softly and carry a big stick" thing, or "talk is cheap/silence is golden" idea.

Positions of weakness are usually poorly concealed by violent language and driving forward, and the skilled individual can recognize these actions. Take a look at leaders you respect or people you admire. Their words carry heavy weight because they often say very few of them, and the genesis of their power is the natural strength of their position and preparations, not their chosen communication methods.

In our own lives, we can apply this same principle. To be leaders, senior managers, top-notch salesmen, or innovators, build up your natural positions of strength and get your preparations for action in order, and focus less on the posturing and media spin.

Modern day translation---Less tweeting and Facebook status updates about your successes, more humble words and positioning yourself for actual successes.

Different ground

The Nine Situations #11

"On dispersive ground, therefore, fight not. On facile ground, halt not. On contentious ground, attack not."

Far too often, we tend to downplay our surroundings and hone in on our personal strengths when trying to deploy certain strategies. In psychology, the fundamental attribution error is essentially the same thing, where we overestimate our internal disposition and underestimate how the environment affects subsequent behavior.

News flash---humans are self-centered.

When deciding our own behavior and trying to explain the behavior of others, far too much emphasis is put on the internal, with very little focus on the external. In modern business, as in war, not accounting for the ground you are currently on, can lead to wasted effort, failure, or defeat.

The term "ground" can loosely be translated into "market" for the purpose of business discussion. How often do we hear the difference between pull and push marketing strategies? Do we let the market tell us what they want, have demand build up, and slowly feed the beast? Or do we push our great ideas and products onto people, flood the markets, and make markets adapt to our products? From a marketing perspective, it's lazy and simple to say, "use both."

Think about the behavior that is produced.

All marketing, strategies, presentations, and the like are all about promoting certain behaviors among people. What do we want people to *do* once they have been exposed to us? Victory is ultimately subjectively defined by leadership, but being able to predict behavior will ensure victory, in business and in battle. If we want someone to eat a plate of food tomorrow, is there a better chance of them eating it if we starve them or throw 20 plates of food in front of them today?

How do we promote consumption?

A push strategy may do a great job of creating market awareness, but a pull strategy is the best way to promote consumption and acceleration, and this comes from understanding what ground you are standing on. Predict behavior by understanding your environment and then exploiting it. Don't assume that your brilliant strategy will take the world by storm and all you have to do is put it out there for the masses, but rather deploy your strategy based on your environment, and you will see how much more predictable behavior becomes.

Make them want you. Make them single-minded. Create the environment where they have no other choice but to do your bidding, and they will love you for it.

Machiavellian for a day

Weak and Strong Points #27

"All men can see the tactics whereby I conquer, but what none can see is the strategy out of which victory is evolved."

Few men can see evolution, much less understand it. The years are short but the days are long. This symbolizes the construct of human perception and our relationship with time. We tend to be deeply involved in the now, which isn't necessarily a bad thing, but it makes the days seem long. Think back to the years you spent in high school or college, and I bet they seem like a blip in time. The years are short but the days are long. For this reason, our mind's eye has an innate inability to process and visualize evolution and progression.

However, strategy is not meant to be seen. Tactics are.

This may seem counterintuitive, especially to all you Balanced Scorecard or Management buffs reading this. "But we have our corporate strategy written on our ID badges," you say. "Most Fortune 500 companies communicate their market strategies," you proclaim. But this is still merely a tactic, one that you have just admitted to being a pawn in.

True strategy is really about the plan of calculated movement and counter movement you wish to deploy over a given time frame, and that time frame can be months or years. A desired end state is envisioned, and the strategy is the path of least resistance, the path of probable profitability, or the path of shortest distance, but the mere *communication* of that plan is a threat to it. The communication of a "strategy" isn't really any one of those things; it's merely a way to decrease resistance among the workforce and customer markets, thereby becoming a tactic. Stay with me on this one...

We have already established that all organizations are fundamentally interactions of individual people. These interactions sum to the resistance level felt by management in the pursuit of the *organizational ideal*, which is the desired ultimate end state of the company. Much like the ego ideal, which is Freud's idea of the perfect inner-self, the organizational ideal needs the individuals to collectively behave in a way that achieves this eventual self. I'm getting to the point, I promise...

The *pursuit* of the organizational ideal is where individuals align their priorities and find satisfaction in their work functions and corporate environments. Communication is the bond of the individual to the pursuit of the organizational ideal. Individuals need to have a sense of purpose, and communicating "strategy" is a way for people to feel included---to feel that what they do on a daily basis matters. However, this is merely a tactic of leadership. The strategy and evolution from leadership lies hidden in the underbelly of the corporate psychosis. While the people on the surface feel they are following the "strategy," they are really partaking in a management tactic aimed at reducing resistance, in pursuit of the organizational ideal.

Phew. OK enough psychobabble on that one.

At the risk of sounding Machiavellian (OK, you got me, but by now you should realize I may possess some dark triad personality traits), your strategy should be held close to the vest, with your tactics aimed at the manipulation and exploitation needed to achieve the evolution you desire…in an ethical manner, of course.

Too many times, we are left trying to convince others of our strategy and substantiate our methods, even when we know we are right. If you are in a position of power and want to truly accomplish your goals, ensure that no one can see your strategy. Craft your tactics around the accomplishment of your objectives and the reduction of internal and external forces that look to add weight to your process speeds, which ultimately slow down the velocity of your strategic deployment.

It may sound harsh, but sometimes we know we are the smartest person in the room. If that is the case, do we really need to explain to everyone else why we are doing something? Tell them what they need to know and make sure they are happy and secure. I would say ends justify the means, but that would imply we are doing something sinister. We aren't. As long as we take care of people, they don't necessarily need to know the end game, or even their part in it. In the end, everyone wins.

Haven't you always wanted to be Machiavellian for a day? Now's your chance…have fun.

Regulated by the infinite

Weak and Strong Points #28

"Do not repeat the tactics which have gained you one victory, but let your methods be regulated by the infinite variety of circumstances."

We hear it all the time, "go with what got you there". Sports coaches love that phrase, and after all, it does have some element of truth. If you are in a championship game, why not go with the lineup or tactics that got you there in the first place? In their cases, they are right, but only for one reason and one reason alone. Their construct is fixed. Let's take hockey as our example and examine the boundaries of the environment. The ice dimensions are the same, the puck weight, player limit, and referee numbers are all constant. Even the temperature in the rink will be the same (within a few degrees), from the first game of the season to the championship game. In the sports arena, going with "what got you there" does indeed work, because there is no infinite variety of circumstance and the environment is a fixed construct.

If only life were that simple…

Everything outside fixed constructs like sports exists in a word of factorials, where probability calculations involve many combinations and permutations, with the previously successful tactic only being one piece of the puzzle. Going with "what got you there" is not only an exercise of laziness, but also one that ensures predictability and the probability of defeat. It fails to take the environment into account.

The environment has as much, if not more, importance to the strategy you chose than your personal capability.

Many of us develop subject matter expertise in certain areas, which tend to become our bread and butter. This works in a general sense, but in certain situations, we tend to rely on our own abilities too much.

We can change our skills, our knowledge, and our expertise. We cannot change the environment.

Understanding this, doesn't it make sense to base our strategy around the combination of circumstances since this is often out of our control? The best method may not align with our strongest skills, but luckily, we have the ability to learn a new trick or two, even if we are old dogs. Does the chameleon change to the environment, or morph the tree branch to the color of her scales? Even if a dark brown color was enough to camouflage her to safety for years…if her next branch is green and a predator is coming, should she go with what got her there or use a tactic dictated on the combination of circumstance? Pretty easy example, but you would be surprised as to how few would actually come up with the correct answer.

Regulate your tactics only by the infinite. Regulate by examining the infinite possibilities that the circumstance gives you, in addition to the successful tactics you have deployed in the past. Worlds are ever changing, and successful tactics will be defined by the incorporation of these changing environments with our current skill sets.

Besides, no one likes a one-trick pony.

Using fire to create

The Attack by Fire #7

"If there is an outbreak of fire, but the enemy's soldiers remain quiet, bide your time and do not attack."

Attacking by fire in feudal wartimes was a way to confuse the enemy ranks and destroy enemy possessions with mass destruction and fear. Confusion and fear were the two main elements of an attack by fire, because it diverted soldiers from their posts, and produced mass panic. Many camps, however, were equipped to handle attacks by fire because this instant and devastating effect was well documented, which allowed soldiers to remain quiet and at the ready. Far too often, we see an attack by fire followed by a subsequent onslaught, without checking first to see if the truly intended effects of the fire took place. This is different than striking while the iron is hot, because in this circumstance, biding your time will ensure you are victorious.

Ever notice how some people put plans in motion, and they seem to have this unstoppable self-imposed inertia? Managers and leaders are notorious for this, and often hide it under the catchy phrase of "agile" project management. The first deployment of the plan doesn't have the intended effect, but the show must go on! We will adapt and be nimble! We will be agile! In full disclosure, I do practice agile project management and believe in the methodology, however, not when it is used to keep propelling a bad plan forward under the guise that we are going to "figure it out as we go along."

If the first attack doesn't yield the results you want, or more importantly, doesn't create the situation you need (soldiers not distracted) to continue, then bide your time and do not attack.

Remember, we achieve what we want in business and in life *by creating situations that make behavior predictable.* Figuring it out as we go along is basically a lazy way to say we are just plodding along, accepting fate that is dealt TO us, and not creating environments that yield predictable and sustainable success. Whether we are leaving an outlet free, or watching an enemy cross a river, our movements should be based on the environments and situations we create, and thereby, control.

No plans ever turn out how we intend them to, at least not 100% of how we intended. Think of where you sit at this very moment, and think back five years ago and ask yourself, did you really think you would be where you are? Some may be in better places, others may be in worse places, but to be exactly where you planned is highly unlikely. If so, tell me what the next great stock investment is, because you have a gift (or you happen to be reading this in prison or some other place where your location is predetermined for you). Now let's think of the variance of where you thought you would be and where you actually are. You most likely aren't in a "worse" spot, but most certainly in a different spot, due to what life has thrown at you, changing circumstances, or new variables to the equation such as finding your soul mate.

Those of you who have let life just come to you most likely have left some stuff on the table, though hopefully you have no regrets. Those of you who have created the situations and outcomes you've wanted, can you think back to the specific times where your actions have molded situations that created your path today? I bet you can.

Generally speaking, people are happiest in life when they feel a sense of ownership of their current position. Planning alone is not enough, because I think most of us have a general plan. Having the ability to implement that plan, and put a stop to it if the intended results do not occur, ensure that we can reboot and try again. Knowing that it is more important to *create successful situations* than to merely implement our plan just for the sake of implementation is the key message here. Your plan should get easier as you go along, because the stage preceding your current one should have cleared out all of the soldiers for you, or at least confused them momentarily.

Ever heard the phrase "youth is wasted on the young"? That only applies to people who don't know how to properly attack with fire. For most people, life gets harder as we go along. If you plan and pay attention to *situations you create*, life should be getting easier as time marches on, not the other way around.

Put away those matches until you grasp this concept. A true ninja understands that fires are used to create as well as destroy.

A country for old men

The Use of Spies #6

"Knowledge of the enemy's dispositions can only be obtained from other men."

Wisdom that seems even more relevant today than it did back in Fifth century B.C. Back in the times of feudal war, the use of spies was an interesting game, because it was the practice of the enemy to catch spies and attempt to convert them, not kill them. So you never really knew who was spying for whom and where the spy's true allegiance resided. In order to gain knowledge of the enemy, you had to obtain that knowledge from other men, mainly from other spies.

Fast-forward to today, and knowledge can be found everywhere. The Internet has changed the world forever, and technology has made information accessible on a scale never seen before in human history. But does this abundance of information give us true knowledge of our enemy's disposition? I'll ask you this: can someone look at your social media page and tell someone else what your quirks and private habits are? If so, then you share way too much information online and should probably learn about privacy settings.

Is technology helping or hurting our social skills?

Research shows that technology hurts our social skills, and there is really nothing "social" about the technology and media we use. Corporations are starting to see mass influxes of recent college grads that have the technical ability to program satellites and configure mass data centers, but can't properly shake someone's hand, look them in the eye, and have a 10-minute conversation without saying the word "um" 30 times.

There is currently a dichotomy that exists in corporations today. In a general sense, the older workers have all of the people skills one could hope for (except all you crotchety folks, you know who you are). They came from an age where social media didn't exist, the ability to sell yourself was the only differentiator, and your word was your bond. The younger workers are defined by the technology they understand, the trends they can identify in target markets that they belong to, and fast-changing landscapes of gaming, social media, and various other technologies. Both skill sets are required; however, one is far more important than the other.

Technologies change. The value of having the ability to know a man by looking into this eyes and shaking his hand will never change. However, we see the trend going in the wrong direction. Soon, the ability to know another person's disposition will be lost upon us, and corporations will be filled with technical geniuses who don't have the ability to order a ham sandwich in person.

Since we understand that judgments and corporate decisions are ultimately comprised of the feelings of humans, knowing what exactly makes other humans tick and what their dispositions are, is the best way to influence outcomes and predict behavior. Data, metrics, correlations, and analyses are all well and good, but how many times do you personally make final decisions on something when all of the "data" points the other way? Sometimes, as humans, we just feel something is right, and base our decisions solely on that feeling, ignoring "information" along the way.

Hone your ability to understand other humans, and to glean from your interactions with them, what no Internet search or technology book can give you. Understand social situations, body language, and emotional intelligence. You will be far more valuable than being a subject matter expert in any ephemeral technology.

This skill set will never expire or become obsolete, and the talent pool is quickly shrinking.

Studying emotional intelligence and understanding how the corporate psychosis and personality is comprised of much more than just data displayed in Internet searches will give you the ultimate edge in your daily tasks.

Know that certain knowledge can only be obtained from other men, and the better you are at uncovering these dispositions, the better you become at predicting and influencing individual and organizational behavior.

Unless you really think having that diamond camouflage in your first person shooter game will be relevant in 20 years…

Deception can make dreams come true

Laying Plans #18

"All warfare is based on deception."

Perhaps the most famous line from *The Art of War*. By now we agree on a few key facts of modern-day war (or you have made it this far out of sheer morbid curiosity), so let's recap what they are:

- Organizational decisions are made by individual people, and those decisions are based on feelings and thoughts.
- Organizations have a collective personality and an underlying psychosis that can be manipulated.
- We can produce the outcomes we want by creating the environments and situations that drive certain behaviors.
- We can avoid the outcomes our adversaries want by avoiding environments and situations that they create.
- Base your level of trust on the eventual outcome the information will set in motion, not on the messengers themselves.
- The most powerful skill today is the ability to glean human disposition, not technological proficiency.

- There are an infinite combination of factors that should influence our strategy, and they must all be analyzed.
- The only way to predict the future is to create it.

The final piece that brings it all together is the skill of deception. Deception can be defined as the act of making someone believe something that isn't true. Now this isn't necessarily dishonest or sinister to deceive someone. I believe deception can be ethical when it is separated from cheating and lying. While some may say there is no honor in warfare, any ancient or modern-day ninja may disagree. The difference between deception and lying is that deception is the mere act of making someone *believe* a fact to be true, when lying is the *physical* act of making the false statement. Let's explore this a bit…

Do those running shoes actually make you faster? Does the makeup cream you purchase actually make those wrinkles go away? Do you actually become more powerful wearing that special tie or luckier wearing those colorful socks? There are many superstitions and myths that on the surface level we may never admit to believing, but deep down we feel that certain artifacts have supreme power if we treat them a certain way. Any hockey player will tell you that washing gear mid-season is bad luck, or merely saying the word "shutout" during a scoreless game instantly curses your team's goalie. We have been deceived over time, by advertisements, brands, folklore, actors, and friends, to believe certain things about the products we buy, the clothes we wear, and the things we do, all without ever being specifically *told* to believe them.

The power of deception is at the heart of dominant global brands.

Remember, we aren't lying. No one is actually *telling* you those new basketball shoes will make you jump higher or make you be as fast as LeBron, but we are deceived into *feeling* that way when we watch commercials and see ad campaigns. Deception is the genesis of psychological movement, because our minds tend to play tricks on our psyche, and that isn't necessarily a bad thing. If I believe this is my power suit, and it does indeed boost my confidence and I nail my next interview, who is to say whether the suit itself really does or does not have a power within it? Empirically, we know it isn't true. We are deceived into believing it, and that feeling or belief is what drives our behavior.

All warfare is based on deception.

That deception is the power of brands. Brands of the products you buy, brands of the companies you follow, and your own personal brand. With low barriers to entry and exit and access to a global supermarket via the

Internet, brands are the only true differentiators between products and services today among customers. The same goes for the individual. So many people are applying to the promotion you want, and I bet there are probably a hundred people right now who would love to have the job you currently have. You don't actually walk on water and you most likely aren't one of the true "Top 10 Account Managers in America," but you have done well in building your brand to warrant your accolades through deception. Your brand deceives others into having certain feelings about you, and those feelings enable the actions and decisions you want. Deception fuels the egos of others and perpetuates the realities they need to believe in order to feel better about their decisions and to justify to themselves and to others why they do what they do in regard to your product or your service. Deception influences their opinion, which in turn creates their fantasy for them. As Shakespeare once said, "there is nothing either good or bad, but thinking makes it so." How others think and feel about your brand makes the reality true, regardless of whether it is actually true or not.

Think of all of the brands you are loyal to and truly ask yourself why you are loyal. Most of the time you believe it is a better product than the rest, but were you deceived into believing it? Chances are, you were.

Deceive, don't lie. Ethics and relationships are important in this world, and we don't ever want to ruin them. Expel from your mind at this very moment that deception is evil, unethical, immoral, or wrong. It isn't. We give people what they need to believe what they want to believe. If anything, your deception is making their dreams come true. Crazy when you think of it that way, but, yes, our deception enables the dreams of others to come true.

Create your personal brand with conviction. You will start to deceive everyone around you, and they will love you for it.

So let's put it all together. The modern-day business, from large corporations to small retail stores, is a battleground. Understanding how people interact with environments, and how decisions we make are based on the physical construct of our surroundings in combination with our underlying feelings and thoughts, is the key to influencing individual and organizational behavior. Plato once said, "Human behavior flows from three main sources: desire, emotion, and knowledge." By becoming a master of environment manipulation and the Art of Modern War, we have the ability to control the desire of others, influence their emotions, and create the knowledge we want them to have, thereby ultimately producing the behavior we desire.

No one is going to give us all of the things we want in this world. It is up to each one of us individually to decide what our dreams are made of, and to embark on the pursuit of those dreams. Our path will collide with others along the way, and it is up to us to ensure that these collisions don't slow us down, but rather propel us even closer to our desires, by creating situations and behaviors we want from our fellow travelers.

We can accelerate ourselves exponentially toward our eventual realities… by knowing and mastering

the Art of Modern War.

- IO Shinobi

www.ProfessionProgression.com

www.ingramcontent.com/pod-product-compliance
Lightning Source LLC
Chambersburg PA
CBHW071755170526
45167CB00003B/1044